AMUSE BOUCHE

Tasty Treats for the Mouth

TALONBOOKS

Talonbooks
P.O. Box 2076, Vancouver, British Columbia, Canada V6B 3S3
www.talonbooks.com

Typeset in Scala and printed and bound in Canada.
Printed on 100% post-consumer recycled paper.

First Printing: 2009

The publisher gratefully acknowledges the financial support of the Canada
Council for the Arts; the Government of Canada through the Book Publishing
Industry Development Program; and the Province of British Columbia through
the British Columbia Arts Council and the Book Publishing Tax Credit for our
publishing activities.

Library and Archives Canada Cataloguing in Publication

Karasick, Adeena, 1965–
    Amuse Bouche / Adeena Karasick.

Poems.
ISBN 978-0-88922-604-3

    I. Title.

PS8571.A74A64 2009   C811'.54   C2008-906194-2

Acknowledgments

I am very grateful to the editors and publications where some of this material has previously appeared: Stephen Paul Miller, Tim Peterson, Cecilia Wu of *Critophoria*, Vance Bell and Joshua Schuster of *Other Voices: The ejournal of Cultural Criticism*, Karl Jirgens of *Rampike*, derek beaulieu of *filling Station*, Tony Lewis-Jones of *The Bristol Handbook of Various Artists*, Michael Brown of *Voice of the Voiceless*, Gurdeep Pandher of *wordCave*, John Tucker of the St. John's University website, TL Cowan of *Canadian Theatre Review* (and bill bisset for his interview with me in it), Mel Berkowitz, *One Hour Special* for Access Television, Maureen Judd and Leslie Valpy of *Makin' Movies* for "Heart of a Poet", Greg Fuchs, Interview, *FEVA Radio*, rob mclennan, Interview for *12 or 20 Questions* and *Open Letter*.

Thank you also to Maria Damon and everyone at the West Bank of the University of Minnesota's "Articulations" theatre / performance symposium, Robert Kasher for "O'Reilly Tools of Change for Publishing Conference," Hugh Hodges for "Doing It In Public: Symposium on Performance" at Trent University, TL Cowan for "The eVOCative festival!: Oral, The Written and Other Verbal Media," AWP Conference 2006, Bayshore High School for "Building Bridges that Melt Ethnic Boundaries: Ethnic Pen Writers Conference," and for the "NYU Crossing the Border: North American Bi-National Poetics" for the Canadian Consulate General.

I would also like to express my gratitude to Canadian Airlines, American Airlines, United Airlines, Northwest and Delta Airlines, Porter Air, Cathay Pacific, Continental and El Al, which all provided not only the visuals for "Flight Plan" but for countless hours of inspiration, comfort and amusement where almost every draft of each of the pieces originated.

And finally, to St. John's University, BMCC / CUNY; my daughter Safia for her incredible patience and love; the tireless dedication of Robert Kasher; to Nicholas Torello for his help with the commas; for the fraught love of Eldad Shaar who inspired much of this work; the Canada Council, Spoken Word and Storytelling Program, and DFAIT for their support; and most significantly, to Karl and Christy and the staff at Talonbooks for their ongoing devotion, generosity and meticulous editing of this manuscript.

For all that is irrationally evaluative;
pierced with interruption, rupture
rapturous apertures. All that is in perpetual dread.
And all that is lost
in the grotto of flexible sentences; of pretext and carnage,
in the wracked fracas of lacerated ellipsis, quivering dashes, brackets,
sparks of embattled inscription

and all that spasms in the stitches of impermanence

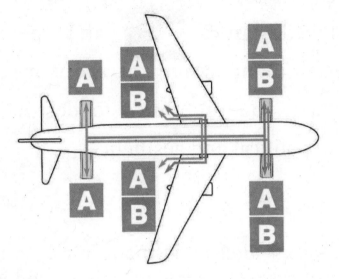

Welcome to the new *Amuse Bouche* 2009. The moment you step inside, you'll notice a host of exciting features; a more spacious linguistic interior, oversize syntactical fonts and bigger trajects. Sleekly designed grammatical frisson showcase a luminous new socio-semiotic palette which features a mood-altering system on all pages; an exciting sonorous service feature for close readers. A newly designed and personal entertainment system at every juncture will take you on routes to destinations social, political and aesthetic.

- *Amuse Bouche* is made up of some 3 million parts of speech provided by more than 900 intra-semiotic slippages from 17 countries in the world.

- Engineers designed and syntactically pre-assembled these graphemes using computers, pens, glue, scissors and other texts. New laboratory facilities enabled the various systems to be tested together as a single integrated entity in simulated reading conditions before this volume took to the market.

- *Amuse Bouche* underwent the most extensive test program ever conducted on a commercial volume of poetry – more than 7000 hours over 4900 fragments through environmental conditions often exposed to narrative deprivation, turbulence, withdrawal and excessive aesthetic saturation to discover that this text is capable of cruising at altitudes of up to 43,100 feet beyond "see" level.

- A lightly read *AB* can accelerate from 0–60 mph in less than 6 seconds.

- *AB*'s potential for meaning production is extensive offering some of the most vertiginous spirals of desire ever incorporated into a text of its kind. Graphematic excess is inscribed onto each page combined with rotations of semiotic turbulence – which carries with it an unmistakable trace of all that participated in its construction.

- *AB* boasts 18.5 mm wide soft margins and-padded information. It can also be used as a headrest.

- Spaciousness is a key feature of this text's signature architecture. Each syntagmatic cluster operates as an oversize stowage bin offering 126 cubic feet of information storage space – especially engineered to fold into itself with minimal effort and expand outward.

Take in the view from the side. Even the seemingly aleatoric linguistic chaos features new perspectives repositioned with culturally saturated foundations of meaning production. Or drop by the strikingly designed textual conglomerate located midway through grammatical cabinetry. Thousands of sparks of light are programmed to adjust service activities depending on your psycho-social state of engagement.

For example, font size and alphabetic texture ease you through difficult moments minimizing discomfort and keeping you in sync through socio-political or aesthetic changes.

Don't be frustrated.

Choose the route that makes the most sense for you.  And for ultimate flexibility, find your freedom.

Many syntagms have played key roles in keeping *Amuse Bouche* well ahead of the curve and provided readers with an entirely new reading experience. From the development of new ideas and a line by line technology, full of transformational ideologies, a lexical overlapping which runs through a doubled discourse of contingency wrought with a radical

historiography, and rearticulated
through iterative returns and
indeterminacy, it's a tremendous team
effort all around that can help you
journey through countless worlds, para-
digms from virtually every corner
of a suturistic socio-philosophic
semiologic system.

TALK ABOUT A GROUP EFFORT: THIS
DRAMATIC MAKEOVER IS A LITERARY
INITIATIVE THAT INCLUDES
PHILOSOPHIC AND LINGUISTIC
MECHANICS AND TECHNICIANS WHO
DISMANTLE OLD TEXTS OLD WORN
OUT MYTHOLOGIES, METHODOLOGIES,
IDEOLOGIES TO ENHANCE THE
POETIC EXPERIENCE OF PROVIDING
READERS WITH CHOICE,
FLEXIBILITY AND MILD
TURBULENCE INITIATING INNOVATIVE
INTRASEMIOTIC PRODUCTIVITY

Countless syntagms have been gearing up for their placement in *AB*. Engineers have ensured that specifications are met. These words have undergone extensive hands-on training, editing, re-vision to prepare for their final arrival. Strategic placement &

surprise infusion management ensure that all the necessary parts of speech have been drawn on for the new text. Lots of behind-the-scenes ideologues have been implemented and seemingly hazardous access holes are adequately pressurized so that countless poetic processes can be enjoyed.

Over the years, we've built up an enviable record as a confusing and difficult poesis connecting textemes from almost every corner of language use. And, through a constant unraveling and err pressured poetic praxis of adaptation, production, rhetorical disjunction, it aims to meet the needs of readers. This has been our strength over many decades and we will continue to do so each and every day.

But, there's much more to today's *Amuse Bouche*. Aporitic & interstitial transports wing their way through otherness & *verfremdungseffekt*. Through paratacticism, pata-gramaticism, juxtaposition and slippage, with *AB* you are able to fly *away* and *into* destinations of confusion and desire – where dreams come and go; where imagination of prospects, possibilities, displacement, investment, excess and liaison all remain a vital praxis.

So, all flarffed up, sucked dry, full of persistence, resistance, this text continues to be made of high-strength luminosity; alloys, plies, plays, powered-up errordynamics, gesticular lineaments which are both increasingly efficient, deficient, full of fassionably fluid circumfission, decision, scission and as such, flies through literacy and obliteracy questioning efficiency.

Built of new materials, these composites – graphematic fabrics of intra-linguistic materials impregnated with proxy, approximation, separation and radical dissemination, form an imprecise shape that shifts indeterminately, ambiguously and oftentimes seductively, resulting in not only a stronger and more durable book, but also one that is also more resistant (*resilient, salient*).

But don't be alarmed. Though the entire fuselage of winged possibility *may look familiar* (with syntactic moments of regularity – graceful sweeping gestures), meaning *will* be able to be produced at subsonic speeds; inevitably soaring towards a supersonic polysemic flambé which will continue to fire the imagination.

These words will get under your skin. Guided by its on-board reader control system offering multiple "landing strips," it will send signals through fiber optic labor more accurately than conventional texts. And, despite all the technology, this text will still rely on a close reader to intervene and take control.

But, regardless of routes and altitudes, amplitudes attitudes, études, you will participate in not so much a period of revolution, but evolution, dissolution, radical illusion, vision, re-vision, scission and ultimately disclosure.

In Case of a Semiotic Emergency

Duties and Responsibilities:

1) See well enough to read so that you can register signals given by textual particulars ie the syntagms, textemes, orthography, paginal markings, as well as the framed spaces between. Remember to also look *outside* the text (if there is anything outside of text), for such dangers as smoke, fire or water which would make the text "unusable." If necessary, you can wear glasses or contact lenses.

2) Hear well enough to understand the secrets of the text. You can use a hearing aid, though it may not help.

3) Speak well enough to give information to the text itself, in fact to all the graphematic clusters during a semiotic emergency.

4) Be able to use both hands, both arms and both legs as well as be strong and flexible enough to quickly open the text and go out through it. Be able to embrace the obstructions, intrusions.

5) Be willing to help other readers towards higher planes, plateaus of meaning.

6) You can be of any age, race, gender, of any socio-economic background. It is recommended however, that this productivity will be most effective to those who acknowledge themselves as an aporitic intersubjective agency of calculation, negotiation and interrogation, a decentered sensorium that inherently questions the cultural logic of late capitalism.

7) Be with no one that requires your care so you can directly and intimately merge with the letters, their physical and material forces;

feel them in your mouth and on your tongue, down your throat and in your blood.

If you are reading this text, you must be ready, willing and able to open it, as shown and quickly engage with the alphabetic system of turbulence voyaging through ecstatic plateaus of lexemic excess.

Safety Information:

1) Familiarize yourself with the text and all its entrances located through the pages. Know how to open the stanzas closest to you.

2) If an emergency evacuation is necessary, do it as quickly as

possible. Poesis should remain full of otherness at all times. If the exit cannot be opened,  go to another phrase, page or passage.

3) If there is no immediate danger, scan the text as often as possible. Hold onto an image to stabilize yourself.

4) If you feel dizzy, close your eyes and return to a familiar semantic construction.

---

* Brought to you by the Lacanian *Vel*, the Derridean *Veil*, the Cixousian *Voler* (to steal and to fly), and the Almadóvarean *Volver*

Econohymonymy

for Eldad

*Come with me, ungentle reader, who enjoys seeing a live texteme inflated and
kicked around like a soccer football; reader, who likes, of a Sunday morning
on her way to or from imprisoned meaning, to poke her stick or direct her
spittle at a poor syntactic cluster; come ...*

come now
into the glowing tenebrae
vexed aria of secret wounds,
archaic traces
of appearance, where
danger lurks
through your mouth's
silhouette

Follow me into this crossword
of dreams, shouts
sufferings, pleadings
resistances & dwell in the terror of
the thickness of desire in the loom of this
legacy mired in the imprint of
history

And, as identity renegotiated
as restaged aegis, tell me,
who yields authority when all is inherently relational?
Who is archiving
in this lingua groaning so raw
and delayed in the scriptless present tense
pulsing in the aporias aboreals licking tongue searing
speaking with flesh.

Come now, with me into this veritas erratas
fissured reverence for all that is
uncontainable. i taste u in these words
immensely unavowable, through these deadly corridors
presentiments of desire

through the confrontation of appropriative exegesis,
(disoriented gestures mocking
moments ringing with fear echoes and suspense),

that moan and cough, shiver in my embrace

And, i am writing now circumnavigating this divide –

in the fragile horror of possibility –

through weft heft whet with weeping muck
which ripples through warped origins,
through the presentiment of
substrate sea signs sides currents
screens sobs. As i invent
this inheritance. As you
keep yourself from me, obediently i wait
in the noonday deixis
through these shuddering letters, points, absences
subterfuge, stratagems

And begin again with vertiginous
imminence meticulous casts
slips, scission, fission, fractures

and turn away / toward you
with secret urgency, unreason,
cut into &
bare all that is verboten, verbose, bordered, burdened, blurred

And in this haunting you are redoubled
in my lungs surging with
your body there
never ending
nearby and redoubled
nearby and untouchable
i follow you into systems of remissions, admissions
inter-missions, markings,
betrayals and embezzlements,
through curvatures, pericopes of
obscurity and conflation, fusion into and across
the trace of your skin, tongue, taste you
across the length of this enclosure

And fraught with illegality,
each day i wait, wanting to
reweave this circuitry.
Each day i am looking for an exit
strategy of stitches signs scars craving
savings exchanges. Each day i grow
full from this fear, this gaze aching gestures of
syntactic tumult, resistance.

Each day, i take you with me
in the spiraling concealment
buried deep within my skin sated salty flesh
searching for the opening
between purulence petulance
sobs ceremonies, significance

And each day i repeat this process.
A strung cluster of illegible narratives

wedged edges
and reach towards you through awkward urgencies
links and perversions and all that is forbidden and unthinkable
forbidden and terrifying.

Each day i reach towards you
with defiance
dripping with secret
blood, text, breath (stirred with strung pleasure)
voyage through this "territory
without totalities," this terror
story (erostory) and
become a fraught marinade
of disinheritance, a legacy of concealment –
wrought whispers, the caress of frictional memories writing desire
twisted and almost, today again, i reach for you

*

And i reach for you
through the myth of fragile security
(sustained through *no easy access*)
between foreignness and
familiarity through pages, pathos, rapture
swoons monstrous confessions
through the literality which is
always the seduction of
sanctity, shamelessly overwrought.

i am writing now toward you
from within this nightmare
of perpetual dread.
Writing from within the tyranny of victimized tropes
subjection, censorship,
luxuries and perversions

from within the obscure shadow of
twisted history,
forbidden beauty –
an illusory lexicology of false premise, permittance

And as i lay down
in the profanity of clattering syntax,
each letter convulsing with secrets,
is employed with exquisite care like pillars of fire in the far-flung
system of meaning.

Each letter,
mysterious, majestic and ceremonious;
like a day which includes *all* the days and *all* the nights
and *all* the bodies and games and frivolity and vulgarity
and grandeur

a palace (*plais*) of radical dissemination
where i worship at the alter of utterance consecrated by
quotation, serration
the art of combination;
and inhale you
spiraling though pulsing entrances, exigencies
axiomatic excess, deixis, disguises

dwell *in* you

fraught with tumultuous re-pose
reprisals pleasure porous paradigms
of observance and desecration.

And, as you languish there, fiery vessels of
dignity and grandeur, i am with you as you
labor and toil, exalted
in phonemic coincidence –

as these wor(l)ds cut up and recruited,
re-circulated, swell in morsels
distractions and evasions –
remain as traces, questions of filial
supplements /substitutions additions
grammatical axis eros. *This is the key to the
haunting.* The privileging, the peril of homonymy.

These are the passwords
from within pulsing boundaries,
limits which overflow their inscription;
words of impasse, impossibility
cut *off* and *into* this archive, this non-alliance of
defiance, fiction, figures tropes turns
topos points.

Rip open this sprawling
insignia crazed censure
of kaleidoscopic interiorized s'ecrets
accretions, expulsions / the rage of
night's insistence
errancy.

Come dwell under my roof in my stanzas
Between the letters of these words
Delight in the fluid spaces
wrapped in fringed lineaments. Rest a little on the fractured
banquette of cluttered syntax and bathe in the joy of reference
mysteries and exquisitely unravel in grandeur and chant the
accumulation of tender aplomb.

Flowing like nostalgia

And set me a season, a raison upon your homonymy
As a seme upon my armour, miroir
For this lexicon is strong as debt.
Legacy is crude as gravitas.
These curls thereof are the calls of furor,
a flambé of vestments – volumes for
many wrested cantatas of wrenched lovers

Note the fluidity and draw on it
Give yourself over to the resistance of this text for love
And be utterly content. Be utter content
scattering night's meaning like voices upon monads, nomos,
the mnemonymy or homonymy of wet matters.
Be the voice that so rippeth the forays of
festering breakage.

Welcome these letters.
Serenade the syntax. For these signs are runes
whose meaning is

burgeoning in the lacunae of desire
drowning in the foundation of ontological heresy.

So, enter these words, gates of meaning and inhabit a shrine of
dissonant shifts, systemic arousal.
For long enough have you dwelt in the veil of
unnaming

Shake off your debt and arise!
Confound yourself. Embrace the accumulation,
the trajects of affliction, affection, confection

confusion where all syntagmatic connexion is sheltered
within you –

For, the text shall be built in the cite of its enunciation
So, conjoin irreverence until the last stanza.
Let the innoculous arise as a signatum,
as a welcoming and a veiling
of all that is visible and voluminous, valued.

Greet these signs with reverence, deference, *diferrance*. Come
with a penchant for turbulence,
recombination and choose.
Come with joy and cheerfulness amidst the
fallow, flagrance pernicious pericopes and programs, pogroms
sweet caresses and fears,
flummoxed, fracas
of memes, mnemes, memories, membranes
Remember though, it is already mutated when
jocularity begins with a
beautifying surplus of solace, solitude vicissitudes with aching
bondage
and linger, languish in the shifting

And, when it comes,
it's hard to say thank you. It's hard
with vast phrases with textual domiciles, drama.
So, open the gates of meaning, possibility
of aching flummox
corrosive recess
and roll into darkness before light for you are the one to make the
distinction
between them.

And this is the covenant.

As one is set apart from the other
As each contains each
driven by the vicissitudes, constellations
aching with spectral glimpses of this sanctuary
as your lips, tongue, teeth, mouth surging with immensity

How fine are your circuitous points, queries, scars
How fine are your precious filigrees,
plowshares.
How fine to rejoice in your
fine garments, festive veils.

How fine to relish in the foretaste of your coming
inside the ornaments of permittance,
inside all that is sanctified and disclosed
where meaning is not bound to particulars;
to fixed promises, premises, plutards,
but chosen between sites
systems, constructs, curtains.
And, remember these tropes of affliction,
vows, vowels, volumes, as you come
to the tenet of my house. In the bed that is
spread across this lexicon

i will not give meaning.
but languish in
reciprocity
and the splendor of pursuit

and i will not harness nostalgia
but revel in these unspoken
alliances, pacts, laws
rampant *reveillers*; awakenings haunted by the
tragedy of misshapen histories, heresies
masqued arteries, connections, clusters
of interminable desire

And i will not disinhabit the uninhabitable
but sign and cosign in the aching ochos
of stolen skin

as your tongue voyages
through "a softness softer than softness"
(*lips, feet, flesh, duration*) both sensitive
and insensitive, acquiescent –
through pathos, passion,
proximity, distance, indifference;
through swollen familiarity, spectrality
as i turn and return
through twisted exegesis
twisted portals, layers, ornaments and accessories
ashes and effusion

And i meet you again today somewhere between disparity
and d'espére. In these philosophico-prophetical textemes
of ghostly repose and fatigue. Between illusion

Between points, figures, liberties
salvaged languages, damaged flamboyance
inseparable filters, bridges. And i am on my
knees cutting across these shareable secrets
mountains of doubt, belief

and in my mouth
i taste you
like *me'en olam haba*
like a wor(l)d that comes and
keeps coming – n'arrive pas
en dérive, revenant –
taste you through these rooms, runes
sites of encrypted scripture
saturated with choice.

i taste you

with the paradox of worship. Carved out of the blood
of these scars, wounds, broken insignias,
tortured textemes, excisions, decisions
revisions

And housed in each word
is the tangibility of death –
systems of coding and decoding, mapping
currents, ciphers, rumpled
measures. *These are the
zones of impossibility.* Sentences
of approximation.

These are the prisons.
The p'raisons d'être, d'e(n)trés,
dented entreaties, entrées, appraisals
of damaged meaning.

These are the
guests, hosts, ghostly revenance
bedecked in reference.

And through these curved echoes, cycles, succulent swells,
rapture, i am with you enwrapped in garments of surging mystery,
cadenced considerations, celebrations, smashed constructs,
pulsing plutards where all is throbbing against the confines of the sky

(November 2006 – June 2007)

Sure Plays a Mean Pin Ball
: A Syllabration

Ubuhubrub
Pingpong singalong
bhangra singsong trickster tagalong
Tictac flogalong suck my dickalong
Headstrong dipthong
Succulent truculent opulent
Bingbang googlegänger bling slinger gangbang

Pickwick slick shtick aint no party trick
Zigzag ragtag petite plotted pocket shwag

Slick lick sic tickler fickle licker
Sticky flicker kicker ad-hoc b(l)öked shlock
suck my slickly frocked bukake cock

Bougie luge juju mojo ousia juju jouez ingénue
Bricolage beezwack, sucker pucker pussy pack
Tictoc kickbox sublingual pop rocks.
Clocked pox mocks fixated pixilated flustered crux, crusty cluster flux

Nascent plascent
puissant raison maison liaison fraison frisson ease on

eunoia blockade memory marmalade.

Flog my blog flimflam rubix fubar lube
bitte bonbon bombast über boob

Sling-back baccarat
spit crock knick-knack bric-a-brac repacked faux fact play back
syllabically plaqued abstracted tracts
these are the stuttered hijacked facts

AMUSE
BOUCHE

(for Chef Rossi)

fuel glorious fuel hot oil and flustered

This poem specializes in small-lots of hand-crafted clusters
and offers a diversity of linguistically designated varietals.
Using the many generations of poem making experience,
it has been carefully crafted and expresses
the special character
of both intra-linguistic indeterminacy
and the location of culture.
Teasing themes from a remarkable balance
of agencies, shadows and landscapes,
it offers a gentle geography of edges, mockery, warped lamentations,
an array of gravelly semes, silt, effluvial fans
concentrated appellations.
The text's different micro-climates and various aesthetics
create optimal conditions for meaning production.
Meticulously, sometimes unfiltered thought with immense character
and boldness lingers
which highlights breathtaking taste –
a commitment to a "no compromise" aesthetic
and a mosaic for a complex palette of
hybrid flavors and terrific textures.
It oozes charm from a fertile landscape of
taxonomies, political economies, metonymies and extends along
a floor of supple sediment

Note: But really TASTE it. There's a huge distinction between swallowing and tasting. The same gulf that yawns between simply hearing and truly listening; between reading and ingesting. Correct technique is essential for full appreciation. With the aromas still reverberating through your senses, put it to your lips and take some liquid in. You need enough to work it all around your mouth but not so much that you're forced to swallow right away.

Because you don't want to swallow – not just yet.

Keep it in your mouth for 10–15 seconds, maybe more.

Roll it around bringing it into contact with every part of your mouth, because each responds to a different linguistic flavor that shifts along varying ideological axes.

You might try pursing your lips and inhaling gently through them as you hold it in your mouth. This creates a bubbling noise children find immensely amusing; it also accelerates vaporization intensifying the aromas. Then chew each letter of the text; vigorously sloshing it around in your mouth, to draw out every last nuance of flavor.

After you've sought out all the sensations you are finally ready to swallow. Don't stop concentrating though. After you swallow, exhale gently and slowly through both your nose and mouth.

Hors D'oeuvres

Oh gourmand! Just mop up those ketyusha
encrusted garnished margins
all blasted and beat-up like whipped ricotta –

yeah, i'll have a plate of artillery shells, with a
zesty bomb-water pottage, a fuzzy naval (base)
with an umbrella of Arab allies

What do you serve at a beheading? a prisoner swap?
a missile launch?

Oh go on, just terrorize my
palate –
your approval rating is
falling like a cold soufflé.

So, just take your explosive liquid
and *smear* it all over my
sweet sweet sweet peace, heavily decorated and all trooped out
hot 'n beefy like a gaza strip
sirloin broiled over a burgeoning cease fire
'cause over here the stakes *are high*,
colossal and strategic
with a garlic-infused shi'it-
aki mushroom
cloud all jihad
and caramelized
with a berry strewn
hez*bollah* crème frêche

and may i suggest
some frothy framboise where boise
will be boise –
enberry like poised
oiseau was o –
let them eat
caked on
Islamist Hamas with side of
pita paté picked a peck of pickled patriots

moistly skewered and
topped with flaky herb flecked fromage
forged with the chaos of clogged artillery
all bollixed up like clumpy béchamel

What do you serve at a statue toppling? a
guantánamo gala? A border invasion?

Just slaughté 4200 civilians
a handful of morphing militants,
4 salted sunnis, 3 shias shopping
2 condied kurds (and whey)
with 1 September that never ends

and ask, *what's in your Lebanese cabinet?*

*Say, is that a raging skillet or
a pan Islamism?*

Oh just suck the savory juice of this unilateral lexicon and
the lingering zing of your saucy

imperialism laced with a tapenade of
terror, a
creamy trouble-scented galette a cornet of
sweet corset a cornish garnish flourish a florette a fleur de
darfur / for tubors or two by
forays. topped with a dizzying *oh mama ma ma sha'aryiah*
of oily *allah la* holy olé mullah aioli
braised in sunni-dried
cabbage, like a ravaged
battalion, wrapped
in an artillery fire cluster
a po' boy *oy polloi* envoi of
honey glazed humvee
with a cup of kaffiyeh
all embroiled in conflict

Entrées

i'm sorry, did i order this insurgency? This aerial onslaught of premature detonation?

Does that threat level come with a side of terror cells?

*May i substitute these liquid explosives
for an escalating attack of piquant parliamentary leeks?*

oh this is delicious militia

SOUPÇON! ... of terror

Accompaniments

So, take that Pyongyang gangbang angrily felanged
dried kimchi beanpaste
broiled beef cabbage fishcake; and *hanjoun-
sheik* it up baby

honey, you ARE the bomb ...

But, to tell you the truth, i am *more* terrorized by my refrigerator
There's an ongoing low grade war
between my carbalicious coffee cake

and my low rise hipsters.

y'know sometimes, after that succulent
nosh o' ganâche, there's a
nuclear explosion going on
along *my* southern borders.

Oh dill sprigs –
anytime is a good time for an invasion!

So, dip your nuclear-tipped
schnapp crackle pop pop fizzled warheads
in my juniper pear jus de jewy
jewy jouissance,

a bissel a fissel
an extended range ballistic missile
with just a hint of

        terra gone gone gone, shia be gone so long ...

Yo, i'll take my rogue state medium rare
seared with a lemon herb crusted
axis of upheaval, effervescently
crushed like a thermobaric cocktail with a
nuclear umbrella –

oh, just a sec, my despot is boiling over.

So, *don't serve me* no cut 'n run cumin-tinged phyllo-wrapped
tank shell
crema gratinata, frittata pannacotta
duck breast con[flict]

(low in saturated fatwa)

no dirty *gratin* scallions, shallot
solutions, because

this is just a jalapeño in my as-

paragus. *i just don't want* no more
kaffir and loathing, punk ass bitch fragrant sweet tease
buffer beefy boeuf burr in my

il fait (fated) froid
gras – nope, just couldn't eat another bite
o' that petit four, three, two, one ...

(KAMBOMBastic flavor!)

i simply cannot *stay the* (4) *course* for that
fudged hegemony high reason treason raison, low rise
maison d'être (**national debt**) no frill fret de floret
stir fried black current. *au courant;*

So, give it up to
drenched antidotes and icing licks
soixante croissant jews and g[oy]za
yuzu hoisin ouzo azul oozin' muezzin
a bluesy früz frissé
for social change
and to all
those misty
watercooler memories for

> The Way We War

⌒

Fromages et Bonbons

Son of a bistro —
i've had enough of yr peekytoe poached dates,
oily baby back mid-eastern mezze

So, just shelf yr fillet o flashy fascism n freedom fries
Syriasly —
Just gimme a Islami sandwich
(toasted awry),

A melting pot of Iraqi road.
A frozen mahdi pie –
fortified with a uranium-rich neocon death trip

A roasted leg of –

Islam is my lam[]
th'islam is ...

all shawarma and cozy –

oh my sweet darjeeling,
stick *this* in your
one-two sucker punch bowl
'cause all this over-assessorizing –

it's just not my cup of terror.

So, don't pull the rugallah
out from under my feat

my arc de triumph coup de
fois gras drenched in a heavy cloying pinot push pull
boor-battered robust zingy
killing field

Put that on your hot list

along with a blackened Fallujian
all gussied up like a gamy-whipped
t(rifle over truffled
toast

Just eat my sushi
with hot wahabi
and don't give me no easy-bake errant
backswing. No sloppy seconds slathered with
a kerfuffle of messculine –

served with a "no-clue" cumin-seeded
macho-chili raison relish
No semi-freddo frontline
marinated
with sweet solypse

i'm livin' large

with my choco al-monde
allah hu akBAR
none –

And, i just don't want no
emboldened blazon
embattled with a itty-bitty bomb
laden with a petite plane platter

no jamba-
laya liar pants on []
all fired up
like a fauxthentic crudité, a
minty monster münster my word,
it's a

croque monsieur

And, i don't want yr
massacred marscapone phony
plutard moutard mouton

oozing like I'rani yolks

freshly squeezed
like a waterboarded suspect.

No more creamy armed forces
bathed in a balsy-osamic vincotto
ricotta staccato legato toccata

all sufferin' from overkill –

a bloodbath of trans fatut-wa
wallowing in delicious mogadishus
strategically plagued with ineptitude
with atrocity

Just tagliatelle it like it is.
and don't serve it to me
as a gloppy googlegänger

a plum palette sorbet of middling foreplay
of immapable mussel and mayo mama may i
soy seared into a subpar fusion
of smoked meat mounting in a mushroom cloud

or an *icy cold war*
over a *very hot*
arms race –

And, i'll take that
troop de jour with a
side of cold fury.

Have a Burka and Smile

Let her dress up like a dog as the cynic does,
put on the robes of a priest like the Alexandrine,
or the fragrant Spring garment of the Epicurean (Karl Marx)

So, fill'er up – buster
fcukin' filibuster
or fill my bustier
as i'm bustin' out

Sit on my f-
ederal bench
cause this ratchets up *my* hostility

and with all that ruffled kafuffle
of scalloped borders, i just wanna go play a little jihadi
and go sikh for myself now –

i've got my global agenda cut out for me
(with my oil of olé, holy hōla allah surly molé mullah hula)

loyal loyal oil and ...

y'know, my camouflage cargos
are in a "permanently vegetative state."

i'm up to my artillery in
friendly rhetoric,
Hamasked intentions – and now

i'm just lookin' for a little over-the-counter terrorism,
(*where it don't cost you an arm 'n a leg*) –

i got my abu ghraib bag, and now
i'm just phishin' for the new peek-a-boo very berry
burka backpack,
the new juicy couture bomb bag

with a truculent and malignantly diplomatic
turban jet fueled frisson
fashion fission frisson scission

My Chanel embossed day gloss
glistens when i say,

"carjack"

So, don't ruffle my politics,
'cause my *Seat of Power* swivels. *vibrates.*
and my troubled Gap Force
is having a blow-out sale!!!

        (*on blasted vintage tanks, hooded jihoodies*)

Kiss my aswad, and woo my recalcitrant warlord

for my A_{nne} K_{lein} 47's timeless design
is cut with an almost
nuclear capacity
for wear and terror.

Do you think high level Baathists
wear soap
on a rope?

Hey, Ahoy there, is that a strap-on "reckless
provocative, dangerous, lawless piece of unilateral arrogance" –
or are you just ...

i miss a "fiesta-striped" color coded system of alert

        (((*without all that extra smooth political shaping;*
               with seamless crossovers
                    for no show-through ...))),

i just don't know *what* to wear
anymore ...

yeah, um, are you gettin' all pimped out, phat and fabulous
for today's hijacking?

(*That's so five minutes ago ...*)

What do you wear for a counterinsurgency?
a night invasion?

Y'know, sometimes, just getting dressed
is a strategically engineered campaign effort,
a grueling obstacle course
of civil intervention / a pilot project
of failed proto-
collars, demanding
fundamental shifts in combat operations;
attacks on security regimes –

Is it all about the Empire ... waist?

So take all that hooligan streetfighting, shenanigans of
laddish tribalism

'cause you can dross him up,
but you can't foil a flippant frilly buster

Bye bye abaya bye bye

But, don't throw out the fable with the *fatwa-*
ter. Take your slip-on
strap-up red hot multi-stop shop
soft Target,
foul pick-pocketin' fear box
that comes with free
boilerplate spin cycle signing statements

And, don't give *me* the purple finger,
my 6-inch "Partners in Peace" Platforms cd
quilquilya in the wild wild West Bank / gaza strip mall
My super secret snack pack comes in all shades of vigilante
minxy hijinx, and lordy, i fear

for all that jury-rigged tough guy scampering about, all
originned-up and flibbergibbity

'cause you're as slippery as *faulex* in a sample sale

                    ((*impeachably clean, jelly bean*))

So, drop the ballyhoo, dodge the ballot
for all this fisticuff aristocrat just sticks to my
elaborately accessorized, high impact,
plunging plotline

i say Mizrahi,
you say RAWHIDE!

It's no Hezbollah cherries –

and by the way, my personal style: Uzbeki chic
meets spicy Hamas refugee

i mean we all want to look our behest.

So, go on, I'raq
the casbah
with your sticky-tacky titty tassle twirlin'

                    Rockettes or
                        Rockateers?

And, just, cool your jets man,
Feel as fabulous as it fits – for whose fret fiasco flummoxes
'cause though j'adore Dior,

sir, monsieur, la guerre, is *de rigeur*

So, take your backless, front zip frisson zone
ballsy blazer faire, blousy blazon
bluesy flooze frizzy zyzygy-string
sky Iraqueting Kabling bling

                    al-Zawahiri today, gone [ ]

How Much More Time

For St. Mark's New Year's Day Marathon, 2006

How much? How much more / how much more time
in reel time is real time between time. Maybe this time you
   say sometime which is no time to Iraq a hula yr
oily slip-on strap-up cross-stitched flip floppin' backless high-cut
   low rise social code of revolutionary curves.
And partie on OUT with yr knee-slappin' foot-tappin' wire-
tapped soft shoe, *no-plan-do* outsourcin'. i know it's tricky ticky
tacky trimmed time tripped-out time / but it is high time / no more
dumbin' down time, goin' down time (pretty fricken flow time)
two timin' tuttifruity cribtime. No time to be glib time –
   osama time, saddam badeedum time
   with yr Surreal Crossfire Xtreme Move-makeover
   death match fit club, cattle drive – (in time)
   yr Battle of the Grid Iron Wild Boy Hijinx Candid
Comrade, Punk'd Jackass. So, take yr ad spyware fear factor
scare tactic, i've reached my Boiling Point / askin' how much
   more time 'til you Get Smart, not Lost,
   in yr itty bitty Bush time – freedom fry fly time
   fee fie foe time, global warmin' warning
   hello kitty kat hurry cane time / there is no free time
   as you pimp your overhaulin' droopin' troop time
   in the outer limits Knight Rider
Room raider, trader, Iraq out baby, and take yr sweet prince
posse apprentice spin city – 'cause there's no more time
   for phishin' fission scission hot decision
   hot trauma in the ER you listening?
This time at the same time what is the "same" time
U R my Most Wanted, you mutant X Ranger trek Pretender
whose raider tomb time so stay attuned time / 'cause i'm dreaming
   of no sky Iraqets in flight
in the superfly totally spy alias [on the record] this time.
                  Peace out.

I Got a Crush on Osama

(*to be sung to the tune of Obama Girl's,*
"I got a Crush on Obama")

Hey O,
it's me. If you're there, pick up.
I was just watching you on Al Jazeera [Sigh] Anyway, call
me back

You seem to float onto the desert floor
In a white galabiyya no one cd ignore
I never wanted anybody more

You're a Militant Islamist
which makes most of the world really pissed
You're on the Ten Most Wanted Fugitive List
But you're No. 1 on mine
Middle Eastern and sexy, you're so fine
I've got a crush on Osama

Baby don't you pick up your phone? Is exile your
permanent home?
'Cause I've got a crush on Osama
You issued Fatwas in '96 and '98
You're the Jihadist people LOVE to hate
Baby, you're the best candidate
Be MY head of state
I can't leave you alone
'Cause I've got a crush on Osama
So, forget the romantic flowers
why don't you fly into MY Twin Towers
Hide out in my dark cave
This is what I really crave
Inside me, make a Holy War
Lemme be your taliban whore

Forget dar es Salaam and the pentagon, mama mia
make me explode like Tanzania

You can hijack me tonight
I've got a crush on Osama

You masterminded 9/11
For you, it was just a taste of heaven
And, oh I like it when you get hard
On America in debate
What a delicious fate
Why don't you pick up your phone?
'Cause I've got a crush on Osama
Afghan Mujahedin
You're the only one, on whom I can lean
My al-Qaeda video star
Please don't stray too far
I can't leave you alone
'Cause I've got a crush on Osama
B to the I the N-L-A D to the E to the N [8x]
To the end,
OSAMA

From the Feivel Gruberger Files:

WHAT HAVE YOU DONE
WITH MY KABBALAH

I

A seller went to the red dead sea to see what he cd ...

II

Where is Kabbalah Springs?
Who is the Layman?
How much is a *galgal, gilgul, golem, gimel*? (gag me ...)
Does Kabbalah scanning require safety goggles?

yeah, i'd like, two Holy Names, a ray of light
and a side of historic distortion. Can you Supersize that?

i'm a little *Klippot*
full of doubt ...

How much is a Mem? a meme? a midrash? gematriatic
address? sefirotic minidress?
What is a "cosmic bet"?

Can you tie a Red thread Ribbon 'round a old, cloaked tree?

Hey Mister Gruberger,
Sling a psalm for me
of surface disturbances
loaded tilts, splotched secrets, écrites, collusions
Are there centers along the banks of Kabbalah creek?

All abuzz with abyss.

Does *Kabbalah Cures*
headache ointment come in a snack pack? six pack, sex pot hot pot zip lock
backpack. alphabetic black smack
My anointment is long overdue.

Whose cult currency
limp interlopery tzitzit slip knot of snaked corollary
scrolled hollers, holy salary!

Scan this

& wrap your Rachel's tomb bling string 'round
yr fully automatic inheritor of scattered disclosures.

Hey Madge, yr soaking in it.

Do Ca(nni)balists do it better?
Late Capitalists?

Intertextile text in exile.

in the K-center Philly fallow philip flopper curly man
of shadows downloads
exchanges

Yo dog, it's *Kabbalicious*.

& who's tallying the interval, the veiling,
the reveille valency, the value
of avarice, veritus
aerator (inheritor) of out-sourced mystification?

Hey mister,
mystify my love

you interloper of
consumable composites, socially soaked
mâitress matrices

mist me
(with an alchemic glaze).

Hey, do you want your "Light of Wisdom" in paper or plastic?

III

And, um i don't mean to "get medieval on you,"
but it's *Zohar-ifying*, this whore text, no core text
cobbled ballet broulé Kabul shit –

(gimme a high feivel)

Do the 231 Gates of Meaning come individually wrapped?

Ba Ba-hir say
have you any []
yetzirah, no sir ...

i'd like to buy avowal.

Don't be so Kabalier about
yr one-stop twist top pop slop
upsized, down-beat, data-based, hyperspaced
bite-sized pre-washed post apocalyptic
vacuum-packed cock-blocked
Kablahblah

(an astro-illogical consumerist surplus of ignoble contingencies)

And sit yr achra down

'cause my *Transcendental Signifier* not a low carb cabled cabala
bar. a free floatin' re-mystification of messy masticates,
cosmically missin' a missin' a mise en a [] mass popu*lie*

So watch the scaffolding (scuffed folds) of
sultry recombinants, the giddyup of linked resistencies and
gradual jams

(*where in Sandy dunes did Kab'la Con
a stately pleasure tome s'écrit*)

& ask whose world economy whose social subjects whose volatile
grinding
wills in the sinewy script of soaked cycles

Torqued for the very first time.

Hotel Kabbalahla

On a black fiery trajectory
Cool texts that are rare
Warm smell of Kabbalah
Rising up through the heirs
Up ahead toward transcendence
I saw a shimmering light
My head grew heavy, (with hyperquadrants to skim)
I had to stop for the night
There it stood in the doorway
A Red String for Sale
And while i was transmuting to myself, i thought
This could be Heaven or this could be Hell
Then she lit a Havdallah candle
And she showed me the way
There were voices down the corridor
I thought I heard them say

Welcome to the Hotel Kabbalahla
Such a mystical place
full of spectral trace
with such a complex face
(a Microprosopus embrace)

Plenty of room at the Hotel Kabbalahla
Any time of year
For there is nothing to fear
a mystical seer –
You can find it here

Her mind is linguistically twisted
She's got the sefirotic blends
She's got a lot of learned, learned Ravs
That she calls friends
How they dance in the courtyard
Sweet zoharic sweat
Some scan to remember
Some chant to forget

So I called up the Rebbe
sd, "please decode this line"
He said, we haven't had that translation here since 1269
And still those voices are calling from far away
Wake you up in the middle of the night
Just to hear them say

Welcome to the Hotel Kabbalahla
Such a lovely base
With so many ways to efface
They're livin' it up at the Hotel Kabbalahla
What a nice surprise
(this combinatory exercise)
Bring your alibis

Merkabah on the ceiling
Pink shekhinah on ice
And she said
We are all just practitioners here
Of our own device
And in the Master's chambers
They gathered for the feast
They hewed and carved it with their steely minds
But they just can't tame the beast

Last thing I remember
I was running for the 231st gate
I had to find the passage, before it was too late

Relax, said the Rabbi
We are programmed to "Receive"
You can permute the text any way you like
As long as you believe

Welcome to the Hotel Kabbalahla ...

Rules to Text By or
Rules of Textual Engagement

Looking at a text first is a dead giveaway of interest.
Let it look at you.
Make that text feel that you are unattainable,
that you are fulfilled and functional and happy without reading it.
That you are perfectly capable of living with or without it.
You are not an empty vessel waiting for that text to fill you up –
to entertain, illuminate or transport you.

You are alive and enthusiastic, engaged in deep socio-political
post-industrial anti-consumerist aesthetics.
You are a socially constructed compilation of multiple subjectivities
aligned and soaring along shifting axes of influence / confluence.

You do not need to intersect with that syntagmatic quagmire.

So, to keep a text from getting too much too soon,
don't read it more than once or twice a week
for the first month or two.
Let it think you have "other plans," other things to read,
to think about. Let it know that it
is not the only text or interest in your life.

You must pace the relationship slowly.

It's only natural that when you discover a text you like,
that you connect with,
you want to read it all the time.
You want to know all about its history, its context, intentions,
peruse its intertextual references.
You want to know everything almost overnight.
So, it's hard to say "no" when it beckons,
calls out wanting you to read it.

But you must put your foot down!

Don't make the reading experience so easy and predictable
that the text loses interest in having you.

Be distant and unobtainable.

It may seem cruel and impossible, but you must be determined.
When the urge to read comes, read something else.
Call a friend, organize a tour, write a poem, go to a reading.

*For goodness sake, **you** are not an open book*

If that text is lucky, you will eventually expose all your secrets,
mysteries, analytic dexterity to it —

A little at a time.

So, don't be too revealing.
Unveil yourself slowly: read it letter by letter,
line by line, savoring each sonoric cluster, stanza.
Read it perhaps only once a week at first.

And after you become ever so passionately engaged with every curve,
every line, every orthographic homage, each syntactic moment,
tell that text — "I'm sorry,
I already have plans," next time it wants you to read it.

Even if you feel intoxicated by the smell of its print,
the thickness of its paper,
the smell of it on your fingers, in your nose, tell that text,

"Regretfully, my reading itinerary
Does Not Include You."

For this text may be dangerous.
Full of unwanted dis-ease, slippage.
It may ooze textosterone, and be disastrously unfaithful.

*

Don't be surprised if that text calls out to you
in your sleep, in dreams —
if it calls to you the next morning
or when you are reading other texts,
or during sweaty discourse.

*

When you finally agree to immerse yourself in it,

explore that text like uncharted territory.
Read it like you've never read before.
Read it with verve, with passion.
Insert yourself *in it*. Engage with every aspect of its teleology,
its material make-up and the foundations of its thinking
systems, codes, queries

Let it swirl through you and caress each mnematic moment

of never ending possibility
with no assumptions of Truth, Authenticity or Closure.

Be gentle AND be rough.

Let it do things to you as you do things to it.
Simultaneously enter its paradigmatic and syntagmatic axes.
With your mouth, gently caress its traces,
entrances, complexities and travel with it
through sonoric and material exuberance.
Let it resonate with you.
Make it scream.

And after, be casual and unmoved by the fact that
that chapter or stanza is over.
With that attitude, chances are that text will be clinging to you.
Don't try to keep it with you by suggesting
you can penetrate it deeper
that you alone
are able to unpack its intricately woven complex references
when you read it in bed.

In fact don't spend all your time with your text in bed.
Take it out.
Hold it close in your pocket or between your inner thighs.
Rub its spine.
Embrace it with you fingers or under your arm.

Make it ache for you.

But, Do Not Read It.

Remember, you are in control of your own textacy

However, if you absolutely can not take it,
if your patience gets the better of you,
if you need to just hear its voice,

Read a little
then close it.

Do not let the text think that just because you HAVE your text,
you will READ it too.

So, if I were you, I'd take that text out.
Take it to a book party, a library, a bookstore.
Take it into a classroom where other texts are being celebrated.
Show that text, it's not the only text in town.

Watch its pages crumple. Turn inward.

Remind it, at any time, it could be
Remaindered
manhandled, manipulated and marked down
It could be marginalized.
Used, sold back or
                    burned.

                *

But, be careful, because when you eventually make the decision
to read the text fully,
you may discover certain flaws –
find things about it you wish were different.
It may not be as playful as you may have wanted.
It may be too full of assonance or its harsh juxtapositions
or collisions may irritate you.
Perhaps you will find its margins too wide
or its lexicon unwieldy. Perhaps its ambiguous nature will seem
unsatisfying, or its ellipses artificially plumped up.
But, you must decide if you can accept these
grammatological blemishes
and work them.

Because that text
is not looking for just a light reading
but a *Real* reader, a *Close* reader,
a reader that will make it feel *Alive*.

For goodness sake, the text is not just after

A One Night Scan

The text wants something real. Lasting.
That only YOU can offer.
It wants
a fully metonymous relationship.

For life.

You Are Advised

I am sorry but you have failed this relationship.
Your performance was unsatisfactory.
And I am hereby administratively withdrawing you.
This relationship may not be repeated.
There will be no credit granted.
No makeup exam will be permitted.

Though you attempted to present a main idea or thesis,
your development was lacking, repetitious,
and at many times contradictory.
You demonstrated flawed or incomplete understanding
of fundamental mechanics and failed to meet
even the minimal requirements of the assignment.

The organization of your arguments were weak,
riddled with inaccurate summaries, faulty paraphrase
and reckless misquotation.

Further, if I may say, your vocabulary is limited.
Your syntax is rudimentary and often tangled.
Your explanations were poorly handled
(in a technical sense),
with recurrent lapses in judgment, digression and blurring.
You continuously overstepped boundaries
and there was little subject agreement.

Though you did exhibit variety and strong inflection,
(I dare say, an effective use of subordination),
I am making an appropriate transition now.

I regret any inconvenience
this may cause you.

If Only
"Patience is Overrated"

If only
i could *locate* you
and your repertoire of conflictual positions,
and remove a thin layer of vacillation
from your well-toned
kinky assumptions

If only i were able to liberate *my* private sector –

because y'know sometimes it, too, could use an exit strategy,
a flash-in-the-pan national release

If only you could take yr explosively formed
penetrator, yr armor piercing weaponry
and sweep through *this* stronghold
full of tasty crackdowns,
tactics, targets and checkpoints

If only i did not need
a cribside explosion well done with
a side of mouthy melodrama

If only what *is* could really be what *is.*

If only these words were not continually retrofitted

If only your blind-sighted seeing sleight-o'systems of value,
spectrums of reference, deference, aching ergo
flagrant aegis, mission, vision, inde-scission
were not full of loss, los, lassitude, vicissitude attitude étude

If only you were not such an impossible object –

exerted through a pseudo-psychologic
legal-administrative dyssemia of discursive practices;
a toxic investment
inflated with no leverage buyout
a "liar loan"

If only –

i could document the drama of desire
in the turbulence of syntax

and the field of enunciation could grow its own truth-effects,
discover its own assumptions

If only all power did not lie
in your stimulus package

& how the play of combat did not always
have to be antithetically evaluated,
vacuously apocalyptic

If only all that was strategic and contingent
rippled with warrant
was not
a constant reminder
to the post imperial heterogeneity of space.

My Love is Like a Fine, Fine Wine

She once lost a grape inside
And in her, it turned to sweet nectar

He had kisses sweeter than wine

My full bodied zesty rustic supple vintage
is a fertile hotbed for your protruding lip
of wild current plum shadings.
No wild cherry berry fig spiced
rasiona-non-grappa,
my bouquet is a buttery, jammy
chewy flavor profile
(*though tremendously complex and can be quite pleasing*)
when mixed with your cloying coarse ultra-ripe earthy elegance
fading to a big fat finish.

So taste my grenache a noche, a niche capiche
Tonight, it's qué syrah petite shiraz petite verdot
merlot bordeaux.
Oh zinfandel, ma belle, bellisimo!
Liquor couture, (més trois amour),
no riesling, weis wine, vice wine, ice wine
muscat whose got, i got vinho verde, merde!

So, give way to my sweet bay of muscadet

which doesn't hold a grape to

yesterday's mellow brunello, valpolicello
monte hoochie koochie pulciano

(*with a stemmy, stalky structure.*
all toasty and velvety –)

For near or far, it's pinot noir
pardon eh, today, it's chardonnay
Don't put on airs for viognier, my oneir
My only heir –

'cause you ain't no port in the storm
and i ain't no tick-tockin' schicker
you ain't no palm-wine drinkard
and i ain't no wine dark sea
you ain't no free flowin' pinot gris
and i ain't no inky late-harvest sub-region of highly
variable microclimates.

Don't taunt me, it's chianti
an aphrodisio grigio; no malic malbec, fall back
fumé blanc swank, frankly,
at dawn, it's sauvignon papillon

sangiovese oy vey, see
you will go crazy

So, toast: a taste with jammy notes

And bring it back to ...
all that is firm and chewy
with a meaty messy nose.

****

Heard within grapeshot

just stomp on
my face, peel
off my skin
and g(rape me ...

POEMOLOGY

SMART, SEXY AND AVAILABLE
GET FAST ACTING RELIEF NOW

Featuring delicious faux fiction, fixtures and fluid accessories,
fleecy integers, noms des plumage, plummeting plutards,
moutard, mouth guards; POEMOLOGY offers a personal
intrasemiotic technology complete with stylishly durable
hand-crafted superpolygrammatic supplements
with hidden adjustable margins

So dress up your poem TODAY! with original shrugs
and reversible finishes, handy logos-warmers,
stash pockets, snaps, clamps, corners, curves, combos
complete with our new and improved super slip 'n slide
strap-on poefylactic device to ward against linguistic contamination
[sic]ness and textual dis-ease.

Innovative and structured, spacious and sumptuous,
these ultra modern pomo boho' age-defying designs
(which hang vertically *or* horizontally)
will flatter your pages.

We aid in cosmetic-consulting and socio-ideological accumulation
with a no-cost maintenance program.

So, whether you're searching for the preliminary parts
or the finishing adornments, let us help you.

POEMOLOGY has it – *whatever it is*

ACT NOW and turn your poem into a new easy-to-carry
polybright hand-held infinity travel loop today!
which folds conveniently and quickly
to one quarter the area of a regular poem.

Available in *Slim, Plus* and *Husky* sizes and lots of super cool
color combinations.

These and our regular weighted poems are available for a limited
time only.

Verbal Operators are standing by. **DON'T STALL, CALL!!**

and receive BONUS superstrong adhesive strips with socio-
cultural clusters and intralingual constellations
that will stay with readers up to **two times longer**
than regular poems.

MAKE NO APOLOGY – USE POEMOLOGY

* Some assembly required.

Tempest in a Trope Pot

For St. Mark's New Year's Day Marathon, 2008

Sometimes it's like you are
playing with full dreck.
You are off your knocker. Fluffed with
frothing folly, you
got shmegegge on your face and are nuttier than a fraught quake.
Conducting with the short end of the schtick.
You are crazy as a rune. Mad as chatter,
as a wet pen.
Baby, you are like a skewed ruse.

But, by the daunt of your flaunt
the sweat of your slough
i just want u to come *up*
smelling like poesies like prose is
swelling like ruses. Come in
from the cold, the scrolling fold. Come
on board, grinding
like a ton of bric-
olage. Oh come,
hello! high water. Come hard.
& come again. Like a month of signed ways

with your beckoning wreckage, craggy
laggage, rag
bag of tricks of s'lick promises
Just *come* whole hog –
in every nook, uncanny,
against the sprawl / go down –
memory lane. Down

on my luck. In my mouth.
Down the river, *dêriver*, oi vei
Sail me
like a hard bargain.
Be my dutch uncle.
Eat my jumbled pie, my attitude, my art
out – Eat my words and
eat me out / of house and homily –
out of my hand, my ampersand, like absurd
discourse. Enter the fray.
And fight me
with furry furor,
truth and flail with filthy
figments. Fill the bill. Oh just
put your finger
in every pie.
Get *in* over your head.
In the offing. In the limelight
In the last analysis
Get your feet wet! Get
your teeth into it. Get
on with the show. The flow
on the road.
Just get it together. In full swing –
And get
my goat, my floating boat,
my bloated moat. Get
to the bottom of it. To the point
Get under my skin. Get
wind of it. Gild the lily. Lick the grill.
Go / in circles. In fickle cycles, murky kikels

Go ballistic. Bananas. Belly up
Go for broke. For a song
Get your just desserts,
for the money, honey –
with nitty gritty brass tacks, black wax. Go
great guns. Go off
fully-cocked. Over the tilled swill, swelling toll
Go the extra mile. Through
the ruse. Go while the goings
good
G-d!

And Without
(for all the commas)

"those tiny rods, mistresses of his innumerable
amphibologies and anacoluthons, hence of such ambiguities as
pole holes in the subject, in the literal meaning of things" (Cixous)

, ,

Throbbing with frenetic obsession,
snapping disasters and the blackness of desire,

she will meet you,

with fragrant splendor, the clatter of longing
and with all that is impending and inaccessible
like impossible blood

[And she is hot and incautious disassociated and
stricken with the blind sockets of hope]

Like shifting shadows of curved desire.
she will meet you,
through the accumulation of sweeping intervals,
saddled all sly and sumptuous seeping though
the sprawling hysteria of
mystery, misery, mastery

Mistress. Mâitress.
Monstrous.

And she will meet you
in the wake of mad unraveling
through strictures and hesitation,
economies of deprivation, postponement

And with reckless ambiguity,
she will meet you
infected with
converging reflection
in the soft usury guarded with
desire.

[Belonging without belonging],

*per coal et commata, she tears
about on the hillside of
language; endlessly sorting &
dividing circling and herding.
She is a separator. A trouble
maker. Creating havoc in public
spaces*

yet resurrected interminably between
pinched gatherings, folds, curtains
indulgences, shudders and abuses

gorged out of the thickness of
enigma
navigating towards
all that is wrenched and rumpled
teeming with indignity –
ground down, dragged out and rotting
in deformed speculation.

And, she will meet you through the perfect fury
of insurmountable grief,
for her boundaries
unbearable conspiracies
sudden garrisons, eros of

dread, sweat articulated
as secrets
without mourning or forgiveness
but moments, moistened clusters
dripping with

the commitment of commitment

contamination –
like pulsing values bathed in implacable
(implaceable) balances
and reeking of approximation.

And with unmitigated anguish,
she will meet you
on the edge of aching torment,
wisped rasps, gasps
groping orders,
borders, pleasure
ports, portents, pitted against
screaming silences
topographies;

She will meet you
as a far-flung frocked supplement slung across
meaning / across trussed up pitches, promises
saddled with
ruffled instances

Meet you, as a *pointe*
of departure, disruption, rupture, aperture, imprâture
resting like the shuttered
night. And she will meet you
between drunken submissions, outbursts,
erasures; between
whispers, scolds and solace
spread out against all that
is emotionally excessive, addicted
to its deficiency.

And she will meet you
stumbling through garrulity
grueling rulery. She will come furiously
as a measured scar

and meet you –
in the trembling ardor of
decaying ecstasies, burning urgencies
and all that is magnificent and muffled
shuddering in the unendurable curve of entanglement.

And she will meet you
through her wracked weeping, through
all that is disheveled and formidable
vibrating in the rigor
of its unclarity

,

and forever remain
an impossible pause
in the horror of your own haunting

COMMATERY

crumbling ecommanomy

comma as you are

easy comma, easy go

Commarade

,’,’,’,’,’,’,’,’,’,’,

commaraderie

comma hither

Fetishized commaodity

comma together! right now, over me ...

comma sutra

Epilogue

i had come into the garden
i had gathered my myths.

i had drunk the milk of definitions and genealogies awake and bound as a text upon empathetic discoveries wanton phrases, commentaries, assumptions and tender convictions. i laid with these letters towering with tense expectance.

And now i am asking, *what* wisdom of urgency of insistence fills *what* power; *what* obscured interpretation, transition lurks within *which* veils and *whose* meanings are supported by this incongruity. *What* lures discomfort among exegetes. *What* spirited assertions of unmistakable promise. *What* embraces *what* reason for semiotic entendres and suffers the symptoms of burning wreckage. *What* sense of propriety prevents *whose* reference *whose* repetition, *whose* binding declarations and *whose* crowning invocations of intimate dialogue hyperbolized in the morning; in the mourning of social validation. *Whose* voice crosses *what* tragedy *whose* f(r)iction rebukes *what* enigmas. And *what* plausible assault of syntax spoils the tension of assurance of flowing myth.

No thought for the rafters, for the impetuous fever-filled incidence. No thought for the geography of fantasy filled with the flowering sense that inhabits fluidity. No thought for the undomesticated mess amassed in the schismatic clusters of intoxicating splendor. No thought for the vessels valued with gasps of skeptical lexicons herds clocks, cloaks, countings, curtains; the final lyrics and suggestions; the empires and overlay. No thought for the chronicling of pleasure. For the idle dissolution. For the way of cleaving.

*

And in the last gasp of its surplus,
i have measured the surface of your skin
tasted dispersion,
tasted the impossibility of pure habitat.

And, in the heterogeneity of mourning,
i am intransigent,
seeking sanctuary in
the migration of discourse
fettered with the fragrance of spiced iniquities,
guardians of language / dwelling among you